NOT YET AT EASE

Photographs of America's
Continuing Engagement With The Vietnam War

NOT YET AT EASE

Photographs of America's
Continuing Engagement With The Vietnam War

David Chananie, Ph.D.

Capturelife Press
Rockville, MD

Published by:
Capturelife Press
Box 2144
Rockville, MD 20847 U.S.A.

Design by Elizabeth Coffey
Jacket design by Mayapriya Long, Bookwrights.com
First printing 2002

Printed in Korea through Overseas Printing Corporation.

Publisher's Cataloging-in-Publication
(Provided by Quality Books, Inc.)

Chananie, David.
Not yet at ease : photographs of America's
continuing engagement
with the Vietnam War / David Chananie. — 1st ed.
p.   cm.
Includes index.
ISBN 0-9711385-5-9

1. Vietnamese Conflict, 1961-1975—United States.
2. Vietnamese Conflict, 1961-1975—Influence.
3. Vietnamese Conflict, 1961-1975—Pictorial works.
4. United States—Civilization—1970- I. Title.

DS558.C43 2002
959.704'3373
QBI01-701166

CONTENTS

National Archives (111-CCV-369)

PREFACE

This book grew out of the simple observation that even with the passage of more than a quarter of a century, people who visit the Vietnam Memorial are still affected by the war it symbolizes. I saw young people cry about things that happened before their birth. That surprised me. I was at the memorial because this was my generation's war (every American generation has one), but why were they here?

I returned to the memorial intermittently, took pictures of some — not all — of what I saw, and talked to visitors. Later I decided to do a book. I compiled the themes that seemed to emerge from the pictures I had taken, added pictures from the past for balance, and showed it around.

People told me they wanted more captioning. Young persons needed additional background information. I asked veterans groups to critique the book; a vet on the Internet said that we should remember that the soldiers we sent over were young kids. Professional photographers who were themselves published authors recommended that I tighten the book. The section on POWs and MIAs is here because I regard this as America's unfinished business. And that's how the book grew.

The book does not, nor did I ever intend it to, portray the complete story of America's Vietnam veterans, their families, and the continuing problems that some of them have. Other books are available that address the post-traumatic stress syndrome, the drug addiction, the homelessness, and the general sense of loss. Some also tell the success stories. My goal was simply to show what I saw.

Some reviewers suggested that you, the reader, should know something about me and the sources I used so we can better communicate in the book.

I am not a Vietnam vet, nor have I ever served in the military. I first heard of Vietnam in September 1963 from a new roommate in college in Tallahassee, Florida. I was disinterested then.

Subsequently, I supported President Johnson and the war effort because I thought it was the right thing to do and because I was raised to support my country. I received my induction notice in 1966 after my student deferment ended. However, I failed my physical exam and would be drafted only in a national emergency. As Vietnam did not qualify as a national emergency, I continued my graduate work in psychology. And gradually my feeling about the war began to change.

By 1969, I lived in two worlds. During the week, I worked in the Military Analysis Center for Bell Telephone Laboratories in New Jersey, had a low-level security clearance, and did some work on the military telephone network, Autovon. On weekends I participated in antiwar protests in New York City and Washington. I had become disillusioned with President Johnson's lies and with how events were unfolding, and I knew in my heart that President Nixon was stringing out the war until he could manufacture its ending to secure his reelection. So while I was not a pacifist, I was concerned about our continuing involvement in this war. That is when I shot the antiwar photographs.

After a stint teaching in a master's degree program that was conducted at military installations, including the Pentagon, I worked in a classified position for the Army for five years. I tested equipment later fielded as the global positioning system, the Blackhawk helicopter, the Abrams tank, and the Bradley fighting vehicle. According to the troops I asked who used these in Desert Storm, the equipment did well. I know the troops received better equipment in the field because of the work my colleagues and I did. That job ended my immediate involvement with the military. I then served my country for an additional twenty years in other government capacities. Subsequently, I began this book.

The black-and-white photos of activity in Vietnam were shot by military photographers. Anything photographed by military personnel while on active duty is not copyright protected and is freely available for anyone's use. I copied them in the National Archives and each is credited in the book. One friend contributed the photo of the Imperial Palace in Hué after Tet. The photos in a grunt's story are from my family's albums; the grunt was my cousin Tim. The photos of the Viet Cong were taken by themselves, developed by U.S. Army intelligence, and generously donated by Mr. William Sawyer.

I shot all of the color photos.

Any errors and omissions in the book are my responsibility (who else's?) but I will gratefully accept kudos and "attaboys" as well.

As I continued to struggle with the images in this book and the issues they raised in my mind, I came to realize that what the book is about is the moral choice people made about the Vietnam war. Some ran the war, some ran from the war, some stayed and did nothing, some stayed and protested (there are no memorials to the protesters), some went to jail, some fought and believed in their mission, some fought and then protested, some fought and never returned, and some served (and died) as conscientious objectors.

Please join me in examining this take on a part of our national story, and consider the question: "What shall we teach our children?"

David Chananie
Washington, D.C.
2001

ACKNOWLEDGMENTS

Thanks to Henry Montes, Daniel Sexton, William Sawyer, and the *Sun-Tattler* for permission to use their photographs in this book; to the Frederick Hart estate and the Vietnam Veterans Memorial Fund for permission to use a photograph of the Three Soldiers statue; to the Vietnam Women's Memorial Project for permission to use photographs of the Vietnam Women's Memorial; to the staff of the Still Pictures Branch of the National Archives for their able and willing assistance; to Jeffrey Jay for help focusing; to Bob Strassman for his initial appraisal; to Owen Touster for his advice; to Ann and Carl Purcell for encouraging my photography; to Sal Lopes for his suggestions; to Jewel Easter for her assistance; to Frank Herrera for his help with photography; to Sylvia Cole for her help with publishing; to Jane Cotnoir for her help with editing; to Ted Clark for his critique; to Dirck Halstead for his critique; to Ivan Hoffman for his fine legal work; and to my family and friends for their support. Thanks to the martial artists, the antiwar protesters, the Canadians (particularly Freeman Patterson) and Israelis, and the teenagers who reviewed this book. Finally, thanks to the Veterans Administration staff and the Veterans Center staff in Ft. Lauderdale, Florida, and to the Vietnam veterans — especially the Ft. Lauderdale and West Palm Beach, Florida, chapters of the Vietnam Veterans of America — who took the time and spent the emotional capital to critique and improve this book. They identified issues and sensitivities and made recommendations that shaped a better work.

Dedication

A father explained to his perhaps five-year-old son the meaning of the names inscribed on the Vietnam Memorial. The son said, "These people really earned their flowers." Yes, they did.

But the deaths did not end with the battlefield. I wish to dedicate this book as well to the memory of my friend Col. James Jay, United States Army. The Viet Cong put a price on his head, but it was cancer from Agent Orange that did him in.

Jr • JAMES V TAURISANO • DAVID R BURGESS J
AUL S PRUSKO • GERALD H GAYLOR • EDWIN R G
ERWIN B TEMPLIN Jr • DAVID H ELISOVSKY • JO
AYMOND L BOWEN Jr • EDWARD J COX • LAWREN
R SPRICK • RICHARD A SULLIVAN • WILLIAM H WAL
JAMES P DONNELL • ROBERT C BOWMAN • MON
DAVID E BURKES • JAMES P COATS • HARRY R CR
EUGENE D DOLLAR • PAUL M BELL • DEAN J ELICH
SAMUEL P GIFFARD • DONALD R GRIBLER • REYNA
N JOHN D HETTERLY Sr • WOODIE LEE HICKS • R
JAMES • WALTER B JOHNSON • DANIEL G MECHLI
r • ROBERT A KOWALSKI • WENCESLEO KUILAN • R
JAMES B JONES • DONALD T MITCHELL • JOHN
EN M PASHMAN • HENRY PASLEY • WILLIAM J PHILL
NE C SUMMERS • ROBERT TILLER • WESTOVEL VENA
HAROLD E WILLIS • RICHARD D YOUTSEY • ST

CHAPTER 1

Introduction

"Let the word go forth from this time and place, to friend and foe alike, that the torch has been passed to a new generation of Americans — born in this century, tempered by war, disciplined by a hard and bitter peace, proud of our ancient heritage — and unwilling to witness or permit the slow undoing of those human rights to which this nation has always been committed, and to which we are committed today at home and around the world.

Let every nation know, whether it wishes us well or ill, that we shall pay any price, bear any burden, meet any hardship, support any friend, oppose any foe to assure the survival and the success of liberty."

John F. Kennedy, Inaugural Address, 1961

Detail from the
Vietnam Women's
Memorial statue,
honoring the women
who served in Vietnam.
It is located at the
Vietnam Veterans
Memorial, Washington,
D.C. The nurse
depicted was herself
killed in Vietnam.

WILLIAM E PARKER III
JANIS ABOLINS
KENNETH L FOUNTAIN
ROBERT J BOWLIN

Statue of the
Three Soldiers,
a part of the
Vietnam Memorial.

The Vietnam Memorial Wall, shaped in a V, is inscribed with the names of the almost 60,000 American soldiers killed in Vietnam.

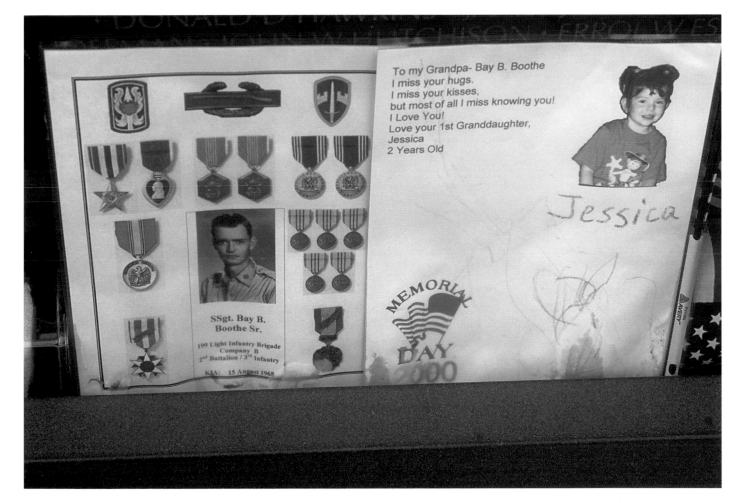

CHAPTER 2

Teach Your Children

In the West, our predilection to commit carnage clashes with our Bible's commandment not to murder. We strive to resolve that tension when we as a nation loose our young to kill and to die. We explain to our children why they should kill or die — that sometimes killing is murder and sometimes it is not murder, and that it is all right for them to die, no matter how much we will miss them, because …

For the Vietnam War, the nation was divided and many made different moral decisions which guided their actions. As our children examine their country's past, what lessons can they carry with them to their future?

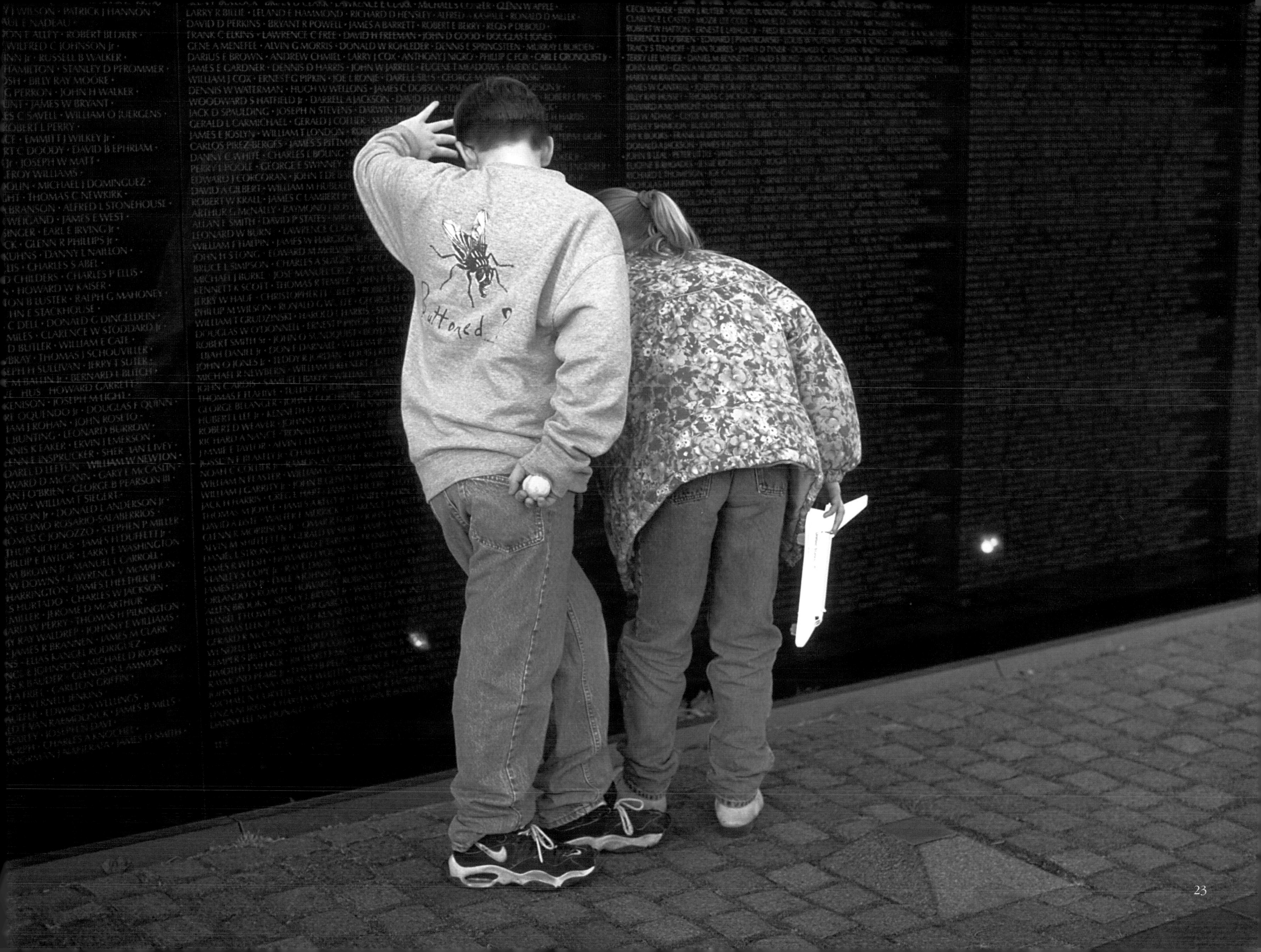

What did President
Clinton teach his
daughter Chelsea
about the Vietnam War?

New York City cops
assigned to control
the antiwar protest,
October 1969.

Photojournalists wait
for the protest to start,
New York City,
October 1969.

CHAPTER 3

Antiwar Protest

The Vietnam War divided American society more than anything since the Civil War. The division transcended traditional groupings such as political party, age, sex, and race. All sides assailed the patriotism and motives of their opponents. Issues of who was the patriot or the traitor — the one who went when called or the one who protested the call — became real and personal. When called up for the draft, some served, some were excused, some feigned illness, some claimed conscientious objector status, some hid, some chose prison, and some fled the United States. Hawks, supporters of the government's war policy, and Doves, their detractors, met and clashed repeatedly. It was a time for making choices.

Tensions over the war mingled with turmoil over the contemporaneous Civil Rights movement; the search for alternative lifestyles; and explorations of sex, drugs, and rock and roll. In April 1968, Martin Luther King Jr. was assassinated. Underlying social tensions erupted; blood flowed; and Americans rioted, looted, and burned their cities in such places as Los Angeles,

Detroit, and Washington, D.C. Snipers shot police as well as firemen who came to douse the flames. The police were bludgeoned. The government sent troops and tanks to quiet the eruptions, quash the riots, quell the bloodletting, and quench the fires. Order was imposed. But the physical scars on the cities persisted for twenty-five years, as did some of the psychological ones.

In July 1969, President Richard Nixon began intermittently withdrawing American troops from Vietnam. Antiwar protesters held a nationwide demonstration, called the Moratorium, in October, and staged a subsequent rally in Washington, D.C., in November. In 1970, *The New York Times* published *The Pentagon Papers*, a classified government study showing the questionable nature of the history and activities of the American government in Vietnam. By 1971, polls showed that the majority of American people had turned against the war. Congress slowly started to take action to limit the president's war-making authority. By

1972, almost all the American troops had been withdrawn.

Nixon signed a peace treaty with the North Vietnamese in October 1972, but when the North Vietnamese stalled the returning of American prisoners of war, he ordered eleven days of massive bombing of their capital, Hanoi. The bombing, which occurred over the Christmas period, drew protests from other nations and the Pope tried to intercede, but Nixon persisted. In March 1973, the last installment to date of American POWs came home.

As Nixon continued to withdraw American troops from Vietnam, as American participation in the war wound down, and as the draft ceased to be such a threat to the middle class, the energy for and occurrence of antiwar protests dwindled. Activists turned to other causes or returned to mainstream society. People tried to get on with life, but for this generation, the tensions of those days, while muted, today perhaps remain unresolved.

Signs of the times at the antiwar protest, New York City, October 1969.

Antiwar protest
demonstration,
St. Patrick's Cathedral,
New York City,
October 1969.

Antiwar protest
demonstration,
St. Patrick's Cathedral,
New York City,
October 1969.

Antiwar protest at
the Moratorium,
New York City,
October 1969.

Antiwar protests
bring together the
young and the old.
New York City,
October 1969.

Thousands of
antiwar protesters
listen to the speakers,
New York City,
October 1969.

Singer Judy Collins
performs for the
antiwar protest,
New York City,
October 1969.

Mary Travers sings
for the antiwar protest,
New York City,
October 1969.

The toll rises
substantially.
New York City,
October 1969.

38,887
DEAD IN VIETNAM

Protesters gather at the Washington Monument, Washington, D.C., November 1969.

CHAPTER 4

Fighting the War

National Archives (NWDNS-306-SSM-8H (SVN)(2)(21))

(left) Air Force personnel
rush a wounded airman
to a hospital in Saigon.
He was shot on a
paradrop mission 70 miles
north of Saigon, 1966.

National Archives (95442 USAF).

"We are not about to send American
boys 9 or 10,000 miles away from
home to do what Asian boys ought
to be doing for themselves."

Lyndon B. Johnson
Speech given in Akron, Ohio, October 21, 1964

President Johnson visits American troops
in Vietnam, 1966.

Performer
Ann-Margret
entertains thousands
of American soldiers
in Danang,
Vietnam, 1966.

A long-range
reconnaissance
patrol exits its
infiltration helicopter
to begin a fact-finding
mission, 1967.

A Viet Cong puts a wire through a hole in the watch crystal and connects it to a battery. When one of the watch hands touches the wire, it completes the circuit and sets off the bomb.

Photo courtesy of William Sawyer.

A wounded Marine holds a bottle of plasma being administered to another Marine.

National Archives (A650025)

Marines in action
on Mutters Ridge
near the Demilitarized
Zone, north of
Dong Ha, 1968.

On January 31, 1968, the Viet Cong launched 80,000 troops against hundreds of sites across South Vietnam, including the American Embassy in Saigon. Most of the attacks were defeated within ten days. This Tet offensive was essentially the self-immolation of the Viet Cong. Thereafter, American troops would fight North Vietnamese Army regulars. Psychologically, however, the Tet offensive shocked the American people by signaling that we were not winning this war. Shown here, civilians scurry past the bodies of three Viet Cong, 1968.

National Archives (223254 306-MVP-25-1 USIA)

Charley is waiting.

Chief Boatswain's Mate Charles Roberson reflects with a cigarette after contact with the enemy.

Photo courtesy of William Sawyer.

Actor Charlton Heston
visits with F Company,
2nd Battalion,
9th Marine Regiment
in Vietnam.

Comedienne Martha Raye visited the troops on site in the bush, eventually accumulating over two years "in country." She ate the food, endured the privations, and earned two purple hearts for wounds received. Sometimes she assisted in surgery using the nursing skills she learned in World War II. President Johnson promoted her to the honorary rank of lieutenant colonel in the Special Forces; she was known as Colonel Maggie. Ultimately, she was awarded the Presidential Medal of Freedom, the highest medal a civilian can earn. She is buried, at her request, in the Special Forces cemetery at Fort Bragg, North Carolina.

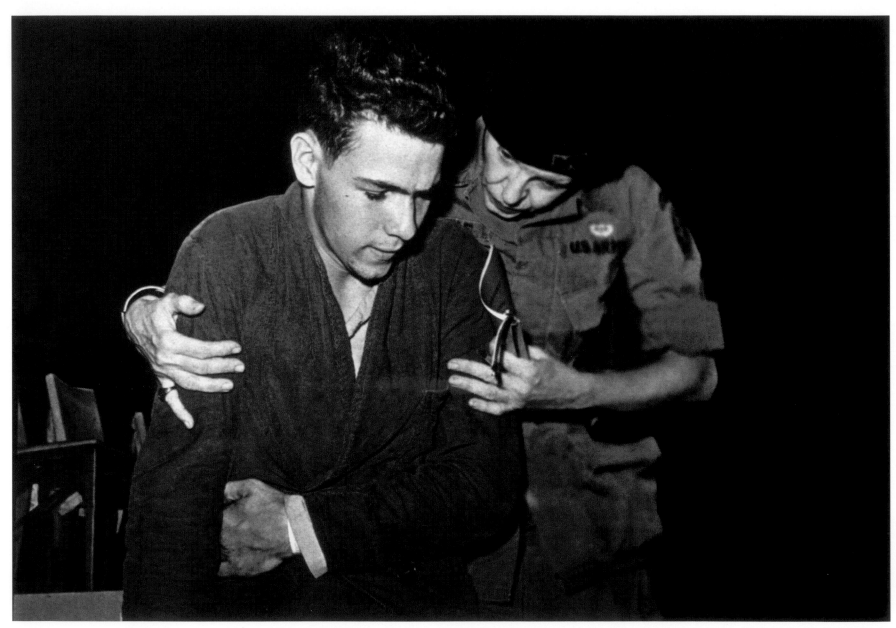

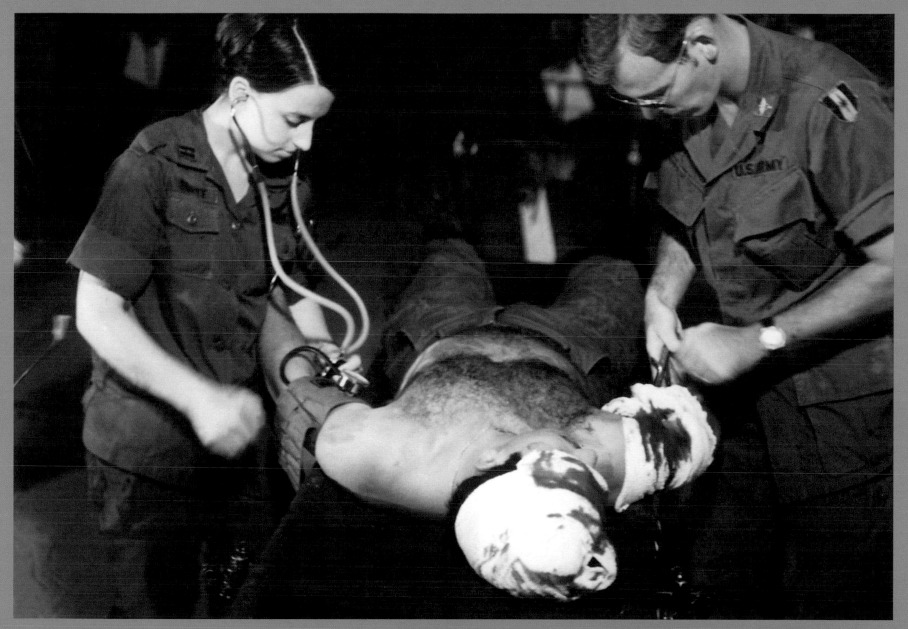

Medical personnel
cut the field bandages
from a newly received
patient at the surgical
hospital, 1969.

As the secretary of defense from 1961 to 1968, Robert McNamara (left) is regarded as the architect of America's increasing involvement in Vietnam. Clark Clifford (right) became secretary of defense in 1968 after the Tet offensive. He was startled to learn that the U.S. military had no plan for winning the war other than through attrition, and he advised President Johnson to withdraw immediately. Peace talks began in May 1968 in Paris.

National Archives (SC 644776 Box 411)

President Johnson listens to a tape sent by his son-in-law, Captain Charles Robb, who reported his observations from Vietnam. Johnson chooses not to seek reelection in 1968 and is succeeded by Richard Nixon.

(left) President Nixon receives the adulation of the crowd.

(right) President Nixon (left) and Secretary of State Henry Kissinger (right) converse on the White House grounds. Kissinger is regarded as the architect of the end of America's involvement with the Vietnam War. A remark is attributed to him in October 1972 that it will take a "brutal" act to end the war. Shortly after, President Nixon ordered saturation bombing of Hanoi and the port city of Haiphong, which lasted for eleven days. One hundred thousand bombs were dropped in December, as a prelude to the end of America's role in the war in March 1973. Kissinger was awarded the Nobel Peace Prize in 1973.

National Archives (NLNP-WHPO-MPFE1796 (03A))

National Archives (306 PSD 71-2446)

Most American soldiers who survived their tours in Vietnam and returned to the United States were neither welcomed home, nor feted, nor thanked. Far from getting their hero's due, some were brutally excoriated by their fellow citizens. But, as shown above, some American POWs who returned in 1972 were welcomed and honored by their wives. The last installment of POWs returned in 1973. Thousands of Americans remain unaccounted for.

An American nurse, Cpt. Elizabeth ("Liz") Finn, provides medical assistance to a Vietnamese child.

An American marine carries the wounded daughter of a Viet Cong to an aid station, 1965.

National Archives (A185791)

CHAPTER 5

The Good We Did

During the war, the United States helped the South Vietnamese people in a number of ways.

We protected villagers from attacks by the Viet Cong, who intermittently pursued a policy of murder and terrorism to attain their goals. We provided routine and emergency medical care to people who had none. We built an infrastructure for a more modern country while preserving Vietnamese cultural treasures. We cared for orphans, and we welcomed Vietnamese refugees to a new home in America.

As President Johnson stated: "In that region there is nothing that we covet. There is nothing we seek. There is no territory or no military position or no political ambition. Our one desire and our one determination is that the people of Southeast Asia be left in peace to work out their own destinies in their own ways." (Press conference, March 13, 1965)

American soldiers
guard Vietnamese
farmers against attack
by the Viet Cong so
that the farmers can
harvest and keep
their food, 1965.

An American
corpsman treats
and tries to console
a Vietnamese child
who just saw his
mother murdered by
the Viet Cong, 1968.

National Archives (A185862)

National Archives (A190298)

During the Tet offensive of 1968, the Viet Cong made a last stand around the Imperial Palace in Hué. While American forces had to destroy most of the city to extirpate the Viet Cong there, they did their utmost to preserve the Imperial Palace. Their success is evident in this photo, which shows the Imperial Palace in 1968 after Tet. But the Americans paid the price in time, blood, and lives.

Photograph courtesy of Henry Montes.

In 1975, North Vietnamese forces rolled over the South Vietnamese Army and reunited the country by military conquest. Two hundred thirty thousand South Vietnamese were able to flee and immigrated to the United States. A Vietnam evacuee worries while awaiting further transport in the Philippines, 1975.

National Archives (No. 1163012)

For several years after 1975, people tried to escape from Vietnam in small boats. The *USS Wabash* picked up twenty-eight people from a wooden boat. At left, a refugee woman cares for three kids on the *Wabash* in the South China Sea, 1979.

National Archives (428-GX-Box 745-1176806)

The triple-canopy jungle could absorb artillery attacks in the upper canopy, leaving troops on the ground unharmed. The solution — to destroy the trees — meant using cancer-causing chemicals, which harmed American soldiers and has caused continuing health problems for the Vietnamese. Above, an American helicopter sprays Agent Orange as part of a defoliation project that destroyed 10 percent of South Vietnam's trees, 1969.

The 1950s American government meddled in Vietnam. America paid for France's war to reestablish its colony there. After France lost to the North Vietnamese Communists, a deposed Vietnamese emperor appointed Ngo Dinh Diem president. Diem subsequently rigged an election in South Vietnam to legitimate his presidency, and America endorsed him. Later, he was murdered in a coup by South Vietnamese generals who overthrew the government with the prior approval of America's Kennedy administration. At right, President Dwight Eisenhower warmly welcomes Diem to Washington, 1957.

National Archives (USIA 57-8599)

CHAPTER 6
The Bad We Did

T he U.S. government did a number of bad things in Vietnam and Cambodia.

We meddled in the internal politics of Vietnam — first supporting France's war there, next supporting an unpopular government, and then approving a coup to overthrow that same government — before we took up arms ourselves. We defoliated the trees with poisons that harmed our own soldiers as well as unborn generations of Vietnamese. The Central Intelligence Agency oversaw the Phoenix program, which selectively murdered Vietnamese citizens — at least eight hundred murders were acknowledged — to eliminate suspected and known Viet Cong leaders. We secretly violated the neutrality of Cambodia by bombing Viet Cong supply lines, and then we openly invaded Cambodia in pursuit of the Vietnamese enemy. The invasion led to severe repercussions for the Cambodian people.

In My Lai, American troops raped, murdered, and burned Vietnamese civilians, including children, and the U.S. Army knowingly covered up the atrocities. My Lai showed forever that an average cross-section of American male teenagers, under the right circumstances — with the proper training, motivation, and leadership — will behave just like Nazis. We are not immune, and we should beware whenever we "let slip the dogs of war."

MY LAI

On March 16, 1968, American troops surrounded a hamlet known as My Lai 4, gathered the villagers together, interrogated them, raped the women and children, murdered them, and torched the buildings. Estimates of the number of people murdered range from 200 to 700. The affair lasted about four hours, ending only when Warrant Officer Hugh Thompson, a pilot supporting the broader operation, landed his helicopter between the killers and the fleeing villagers and faced down the American murderers. The U.S. Army covered up the killings.

The massacre was not revealed until a year later, after a reporter tried to spark an investigation and an Army photographer who accompanied the killers sold the color pictures he took to a magazine. The black-and-white photos he took remained government property. My Lai quickly became the most notorious American military atrocity of the war.

The timing of the revelation, November 13, 1969, was exquisite as it strengthened the impact of the news. It happened between the nationwide Moratorium demonstration on October 15, 1969, and the antiwar demonstration in Washington, D.C. on November 15, 1969. News of the atrocity convinced a lot of Americans that we weren't always the good guys we thought we were.

An official Army investigation yielded a list of thirty people, mostly officers, who knew about the atrocities, and it led to the court martial of only one man, the most junior officer. Sentenced to life imprisonment after conviction by the court martial, he was paroled by President Nixon in November 1974 after serving three days in a military jail and three years under house arrest during appeals.

On March 6, 1998, the Army awarded the Soldier's Medal to Warrant Officer Thompson; to Lawrence Colburn, the helicopter gunner; and to Glenn Andreatta, the helicopter crew chief, for gallantry.

American soldiers interrogate My Lai villagers to gain intelligence about the enemy.

National Archives (NWDNS-319-MYP)

A soldier brings a
reluctant villager to
a gathering point.

Soldiers get to know one of the My Lai village kids before the murdering starts.

Adults and children
are collected.

Torching a hut
in My Lai.

Corpses and My Lai
village burn.

"Travel to foreign
lands, Meet exotic
people, And kill them."
(T-Shirt Slogan)

"How many times do
I have to tell you: 'First
it's rape, then pillage,
and then burn.'"
(Vietnam-era joke)

CAMBODIA

National Archives (111-GTC Box 1)

The North Vietnamese used Cambodian territory for logistics and resupply. The Cambodians either colluded in, ignored, or were powerless to prevent these activities. In 1969, President Nixon violated Cambodia's neutrality by secretly bombing North Vietnamese supply lines in that country. In 1970, he invaded Cambodia with American troops. After destroying substantial enemy supplies, the Americans left Cambodia. The incursion, however, had strong repercussions. In America, widespread protests occurred, one of which left four students dead at the hands of the National Guard at Kent State University. In Cambodia, the government toppled, ultimately enabling the Cambodian Communists, the Khmer Rouge, to take over. While in power, the Communists murdered one-third of the Cambodian population. In one of history's great ironies, the Vietnamese Communists, once they had reconquered their country, invaded Cambodia to drive the Cambodian Communists from power. Above, American troops in Cambodia pose with some of the enemy's supplies they captured, 1970.

Donated by
Temple Emanuel Golden Age Club
Newton, Mass.
1966

(left) Jews pray at the Kol Nidre service on Yom Kippur, the Day of Atonement, the holiest day of the Jewish calendar. On that day, according to the Jewish religion, God inscribes the names of who shall live and who shall die in the coming year, 1966.

(right) Troops taking their first bath after ten days in the bush, using water poured from a helmet. Pulled back for a rest, the unit remained on thirty-minute alert, 1966.

National Archives (111-CCV-377)

CHAPTER 7

Who We Were

About 2.6 million men served in South Vietnam itself, and 40 to 60 percent of them were placed in harm's way. Roughly 7,500 women served in Vietnam; most, but by no means all, were nurses.

The soldiers who went to Vietnam were by no means a representative cross-section of the nation. The upper class and the upper middle class opted out of the war. The Selective Service System, which ran the draft, gave deferments to college-bound young men, undergraduates, and postgraduates because they were deemed more important to the larger national interest. About three-quarters of the soldiers in Vietnam were volunteers. Few among the rich volunteered. In effect, the advantaged sent the disadvantaged to do their fighting for them, the kind of disparity that caused riots during the Civil War.

American soldiers in Vietnam were young kids; the average age was nineteen. By racial classification, 88 percent were white, 11 percent black, and 1 percent "other." Hispanics were classified as whites. By religion, most were of some Protestant denomination, but the largest single religious classification was Catholic. Overall, they died pretty much in proportion to their demographics.

One of the misguided social engineering programs of the era, called Project 100,000, required the armed forces to accept draftees and volunteers who scored lowest on the Armed Forces Qualifications Test, which was given to all enlistees. People who scored twenty or less out of one hundred points on the test — people who ordinarily would be excluded — were included. The rationale for the program was that experience in the military would somehow prepare these people to compete better in the world when they completed their service. Actually, the Project 100,000 soldiers tended to get assigned to combat units where more of the casualties took place.

Joe Leader reads
a letter from home
after finishing a
mission, 1967.

Troops attend a
Thanksgiving service
before going on a
mission, 1967.

Chaplain Habiby
baptizes Sgt. Severa
Jones in the Cambo
River, south of the
Demilitarized Zone,
on the eleventh
day of the Tet
offensive, 1968.

ONE GRUNT'S STORY

Timothy Sexton was the oldest of four boys.

He treasured his car.

Tim's passion was cars and fixing them.

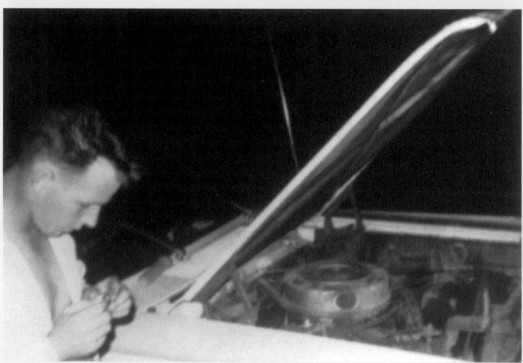

Tim was drafted into the U.S. Army and went to
basic training at Fort Jackson, South Carolina.

After advanced training, Tim was assigned to
Vietnam. He had a farewell party in the
backyard of the house he grew up in.

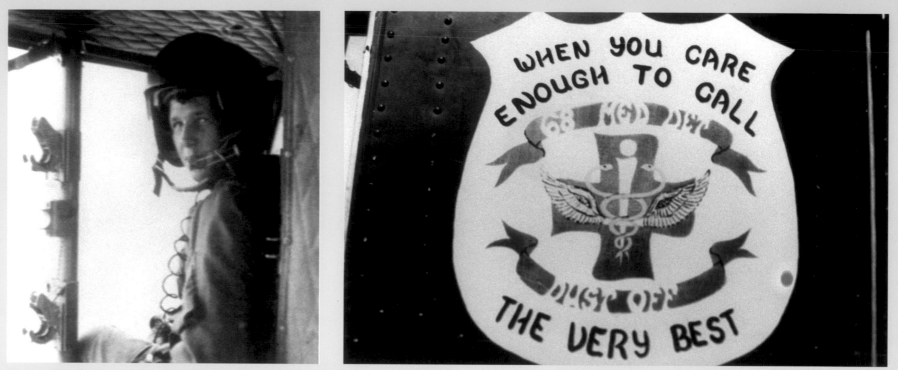

Tim served as a crew chief in medevac helicopters …

and served ably as a soldier.

In Nam, Tim liked to read the news from his hometown, and he liked to play.

Tim came home and disliked the protesters he found. He was photographed as an unidentified veteran by his hometown newspaper while watching one of the antiwar demonstrations, October 15, 1969. (Courtesy *Sun-Sentinel*)

Tim Sexton drowned in a scuba diving accident within a year of his return home.

Photo courtesy of William Sawyer.

The Viet Cong travel light. They carry their rice ration in the white devices slung about their shoulders. The rice will be cooked later in the field mess.

CHAPTER 8

Who They Were

The Viet Cong took these photographs themselves. The American military routinely developed and analyzed captured films for intelligence information. The pictures here are unclassified photographs that a former military intelligence member brought home.

A Viet Cong cook
prepares rice balls
in the field mess.

Photo courtesy of William Sawyer.

The Viet Cong here (below) are using a weapon scavenged from the French.

Photos courtesy of William Sawyer.

The Viet Cong fire a mortar.

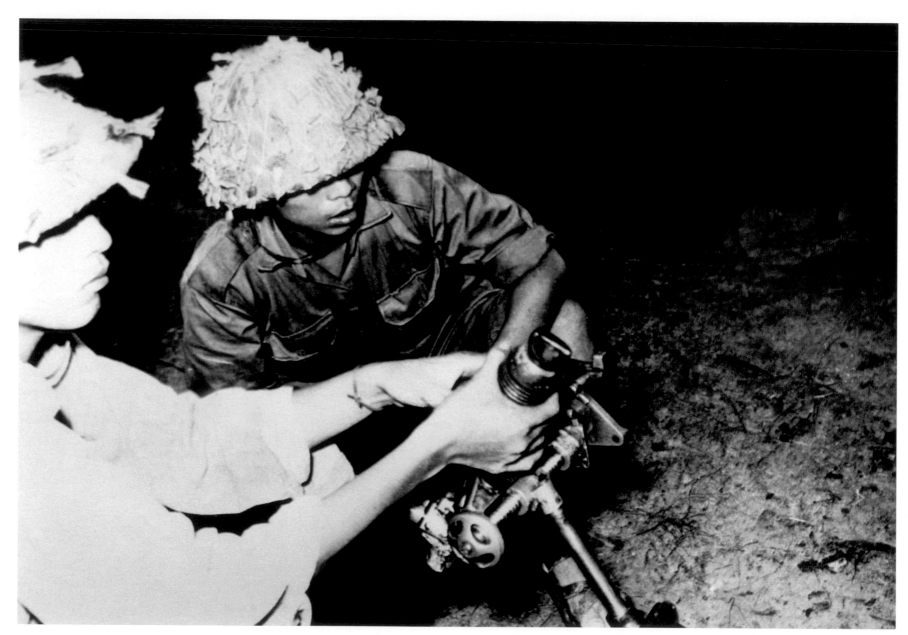

Photo courtesy of William Sawyer.

Viet Cong entertainers dance for the Viet Cong troops.

Photo courtesy of William Sawyer.

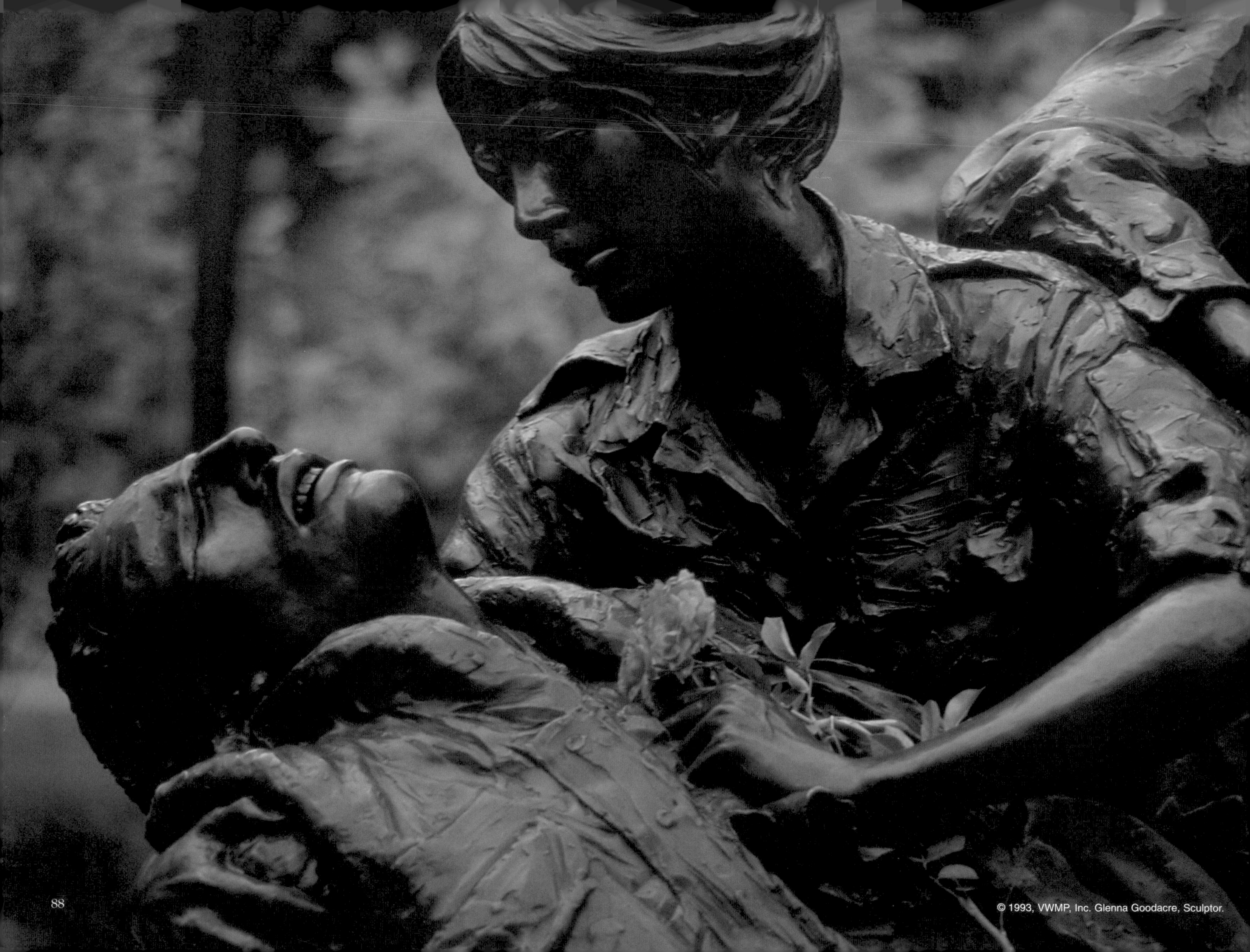

CHAPTER 9

A Place to Meet and to Heal

The Vietnam Memorial is sited on land donated by Congress but paid for by contributions from the American people. Several hundreds of architects and designers competed to determine what it would look like. A young architecture student named Maya Lin won the competition with a simple design of two abutting wedges of black marble inscribed with the names of the soldiers who were killed in Vietnam. "The Wall," as it is now called, was dedicated on Veterans Day, 1982. A composition of the statues of three soldiers, by Frederick Hart, was added nearby in 1984; nine years later another set of statuary, the Vietnam Women's Memorial, by Glenna Goodacre, honoring the women who served in Vietnam, was situated close by. One of the purposes of the memorial is to provide a place where Vietnam veterans can meet and lay down the burdens of the past. Another is to provide an educational opportunity for future generations to learn about the war. More people visit the Vietnam Memorial than any other monument in Washington, D.C. On any given day, you can hear languages from around the world spoken there.

The inexperienced FNG was the "F___ing New Guy" most recently assigned to a unit. Before becoming friendly with the FNG, experienced personnel would hang back to see if the FNG would live out the week or get wasted quickly. They saw little point in making an emotional investment in someone who would soon be dead or could get them killed. The government rotated individuals instead of units to save money. This practice was the opposite of what was done in World War II and contrary to everything known about why men fight in war — to protect those in their small unit who protect them.

"Welcome home, Bro" was the theme for the Memorial Day ceremonies at the Wall, 1998. People just turned and hugged.

Jan Scruggs addresses a Memorial Day audience at the Vietnam Memorial on the Mall in Washington, D.C., 1999. He believed there should be a memorial to soldiers who died in Vietnam, and he made it happen.

Christmas cards
to the dead,
December 25, 1999.

Christmas Day, 1999.
They had left a
wreath at the Wall
the night before.

97

People make
rubbings of the
names on the Wall.

Christos Cotsakos,
a decorated veteran,
delivers the keynote
speech at the Wall,
Memorial Day, 2000.

"*Tired*"

Please God Let Me Rest

I'm Tired of Fighting

I'm Tired of Running

I'm Tired of Hiding

I'm Tired of Fear

I'm So Tired God

Please Let Me Rest

By
Keith A. Decker

You Are never forgotten

May 10, 2000

Dear Flop,

I'm writing to you because it seems like the right thing to do. I didn't want to leave you behind in Vietnam, but I really had no other choice. I told you where I was going and I know you understood. I know you wanted to go home with me, please forgive me. I thought you'd be coming home someday. Had I had any idea the military had no intention of bringing you and the others back home, I never would have left you. The way you looked into my eyes; I really believe you were reading my mind. Coming home was great, but knowing you were still over there bothered me a lot. All these years, I never knew what had happened to you and there was never anyone to talk to who would truly understand what I was going through.

Well, after 30 years I finally know the rest of the story. It took your new handler two weeks to get in on you, but you finally gave in and let him take you out. This was the fifth handler for you in Vietnam and you accepted him. After four months he was sent home and you were left alone again. PhuCat closed on Christmas Eve and you were sent to Cam Ranh Bay.

At Cam Ranh Bay you wanted nothing to do with anyone. The Air Force decided that the way to solve the problem was to put you down and they did: I don't understand how anyone could do that to you. You spent 7 years in Vietnam protecting your handlers, base, and all the people on the base. This was the reward you got for being faithful all those years. I could have taken you home, I was sent to Travis AB and they didn't have a dog for me there.

Flop, I want you to know that you were more than just a dog to me. You were a great Soldier and my best friend.

Please watch over the Wall and maybe someday the US Government will realize that all the dogs that served in Vietnam should be honored with a National Memorial.

We all love you Smokey A912 (Flop) Terry Holley 1965-1966, Dick Rines 1967-1968, Phil McGeorge 1969-1970, Craig Jolly 1971.

I will see you again.

Jim Hart PhuCat AB 1970-1971

Jane Fonda, an American actress, protested the war during the 1960s. In the summer of 1972, she went to Hanoi, the capitol of North Vietnam, and met with that country's vice-premier. She made ten propaganda broadcasts aimed in part at American troops in South Vietnam. She posed for photographs with American prisoners of war and, most notoriously, with an antiaircraft gun used to shoot down American pilots. For that picture, she wore a helmet made of metal scavenged from downed American planes. Her actions earned her the nickname "Hanoi Jane." Many Americans despised her. In 1988, on ABC's television program *20/20*, Fonda said she regretted if anyone serving in Vietnam had been hurt "because of things I said or did." Her regrets were not universally accepted, and she remains a poster-girl in veterans' toilets.

Reliving old memories
on Veterans Day,
November 11, 2000.

Vietnam vets by the
thousands drive
motorcycles to
Washington, D.C., for
Memorial Day, 2001.
The ingathering,
called "Rolling
Thunder," is
sponsored in part
by Harley-Davidson.

This was his first trip to the Wall. It had been more than thirty years since he left Vietnam, and he thought he had left it behind. He found the Wall still had a big impact.

He just walked along
the Wall, touching it,
seeming in a world
of his own.

118

The Khe Sanh battle between January and March, 1968, tested whether 6,000 Marines could, with adequate bombing and aerial resupply, survive the onslaught of 20,000 to 30,000 North Vietnamese. The Marines were cut off by land and could only be resupplied by air. The North Vietnamese initially overran one Marine position but were forced off by a counterattack. In February, they overran another position, were forced off, and then retook it in hand-to-hand combat. Marine corpses were left unburied for more than a month. B-52 bombers dropped between 60,000 and 75,000 tons of bombs by March 31, and U.S. fighter-bombers averaged 300 sorties a day. Daily rocket attacks and sniper duels became commonplace, but a full-scale attack never came. On March 6 the North Vietnamese began to withdraw, and by April 8 the road to Khe Sanh was reopened. The military significance of the battle (who won, whether it was a prelude to or distraction for the Tet offensive), may long be debated, but politically, it and the Tet offensive gave Americans at home pause about the Vietnam War. On June 26, the United States forsook Khe Sanh forever.

124

Her brother was killed in Vietnam when she was thirteen years old. This is her first visit to the Vietnam Memorial. Memorial Day, 2001.

This veteran pays his respects to fallen friends on Veterans Day, 2001. There were several on his list, but he told me all the people on the Wall were his friends.

The offering (right) pays respects to the two female journalists who died in Vietnam. Altogether, 148 newspeople died in the Vietnam War.

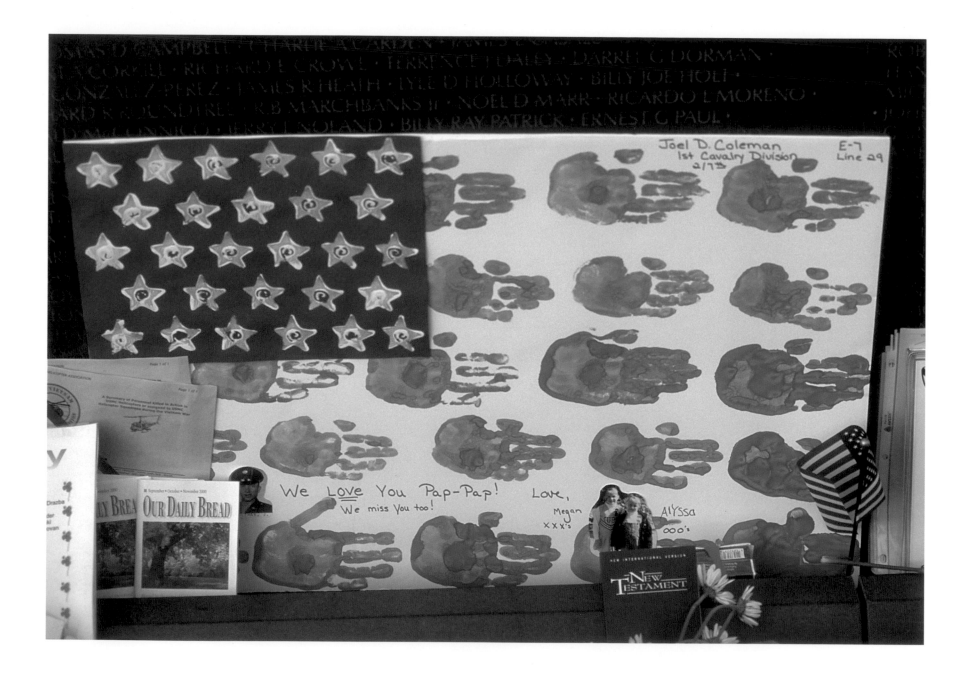

138

Christmas Day, 2001.

For some, the pain persists. Part of the writing on the hat says: "For all of my fallen sky soldiers. I should have died with you. I grieve for you daily. I'm sorry." Christmas, 2001.

Please remember
Col Peter J. Stewart, USAF
(missing in Action March 15, 1966
over North Vietnam)

on his 55ᵗʰ wedding anniversary
November 11, 1999

CHAPTER 10

POWs and MIAs

Not everyone who served in Vietnam came back. The fates of thousands of American soldiers classified as "prisoners of war" or "missing in action" remain unknown still, more than a quarter of a century later.

Rolling Thunder motorcycle rally, Washington, D.C., Memorial Day, 2001.

Rolling Thunder
motorcycle rally,
Washington, D.C.,
Memorial Day, 2001.

THE LAST FIREBASE
Standing Vigil Until They All Come Home
WWII · Korean War · Cold War · Vietnam W r · Gulf War
A Non-Profit Organization Since 1986

Some individuals have dedicated themselves to standing vigil until all is learned about the POWs and MIAs. They operate this booth in Washington, D.C., near the Vietnam Memorial.

147

The list of names of the POWs and MIAs is posted at the Last Firebase in Washington, D.C.

These veterans had the night shift on Christmas Eve, 2000, at the Last Firebase. They maintained the vigil that is being kept. The temperature was below freezing at 11 o'clock that night. The veteran in the top picture said that he couldn't imagine anywhere else where he would rather be.

During the Tet offensive, the North Vietnamese captured Michael Benge, an American civilian economic development officer in South Vietnam. While on the ensuing march, Benge buried two fellow prisoners somewhere along the Ho Chi Minh trail. He was a POW for five years, held in camps in South Vietnam, Cambodia, Laos, and North Vietnam. His captors placed him in solitary confinement for twenty-seven months: one year in a "black box," and one year in Cambodia in a cage just like the one shown here. He is reenacting that experience to raise money to support a lawsuit against the Central Intelligence Agency in the hopes of forcing the CIA to release documents relating to the thousands of American POWs and MIAs who remain unaccounted for. The suit claims that two presidents have ordered the CIA to release the documents but that the CIA has yet to do so.

Washington, D.C., near the Vietnam Memorial, Memorial Day, 2000.

Peaceful twilight
comes to Washington.

CHAPTER 11

Exit

Thomas Jefferson said: "The tree of liberty must be refreshed from time to time with the blood of patriots and tyrants." He thought we should improve the future by learning from the past. The Vietnam War is a text from which many lessons may be drawn. Here is my list: The president should ask for and the Congress should declare war; the civil authorities should define the objectives of the war and allow the military forces to execute it without being micromanaged; we should know why we are fighting and when to stop; the war should be fought with total commitment, never in a gradually escalating fashion; training, troop rotation, and replacement should be done by units, not by individual grunts; the timing of troop rotation should be determined by the needs of the war and not by arbitrary limits; the enemy should be constantly harried and denied any sanctuaries; the enemy should be pursued relentlessly without regard to territorial boundaries; all logistics and supply lines should be attacked — with notice everywhere that whoever aids the enemy does so at his peril; and reporting the war by a free press should be fostered so that the people may be informed, and the government may be held accountable.

153

INDEX

Notes

Internet Orders: notyetatease.com

Mail Orders: Send this order form to:

> Capturelife Press
> Box 2144
> Rockville, MD 20847-2144

Name: _____

Street Address: _____

_____

City: _____   State: _____   Zipcode: _____

Telephone: _____   Email address: _____

Title	Price	Quantity	Total
Not Yet At Ease	**$59.95**		
MD sales tax (5% for MD residents only)			
Shipping and Handling**			
		TOTAL	

** Shipping and Handling Charges
$6.00 U.S. shipping on the first copy, $3.00 on additional copies

ORDER FORM

Internet Orders: notyetatease.com

Mail Orders: Send this order form to:

> Capturelife Press
> Box 2144
> Rockville, MD 20847-2144

Name: _____

Street Address: _____

_____

City: _____   State: _____   Zipcode: _____

Telephone: _____   Email address: _____

Title	Price	Quantity	Total
Not Yet At Ease	**$59.95**		
MD sales tax (5% for MD residents only)			
Shipping and Handling**			
		TOTAL	

** Shipping and Handling Charges
$6.00 U.S. shipping on the first copy, $3.00 on additional copies